Warner, Rachel
Chinnoda's school in India.——(Beans)
1. Schools——India——Pictorial works——Juvenile literature
I. Title
371.00954   LA1150
ISBN 0-7136-2420-5

Published by A & C Black (Publishers) Limited
35 Bedford Row, London WC1R 4JH
© 1984 A & C Black (Publishers) Limited

Acknowledgments
The map is by Tony Garrett

ISBN 0-7136-2420-5

Filmset by August Filmsetting, Haydock, St Helens
Colour origination by Hongkong Graphic Arts Service Centre, Hong Kong
Printed in Hong Kong by Dai Nippon Printing Co.

Chinnoda's School in India

Rachel Warner

Adam and Charles Black · London

My name is P. Narayana Reddy. I am thirteen and I come from a small village called Chinthalacheruvu in Andhra Pradesh. Andhra Pradesh is a large state in the south of India. The capital of Andhra Pradesh is Hyderabad, but I've never been there.

Here I am with my family on the roof of our house. I'm standing between my brother and my dad. My two younger sisters are next to my mum. We've all got our best clothes on. Dad is wearing a white lungi – a piece of cloth round his waist. Lots of men wear lungis because they are cooler than trousers. Mum is wearing one of her best saris for the photograph.

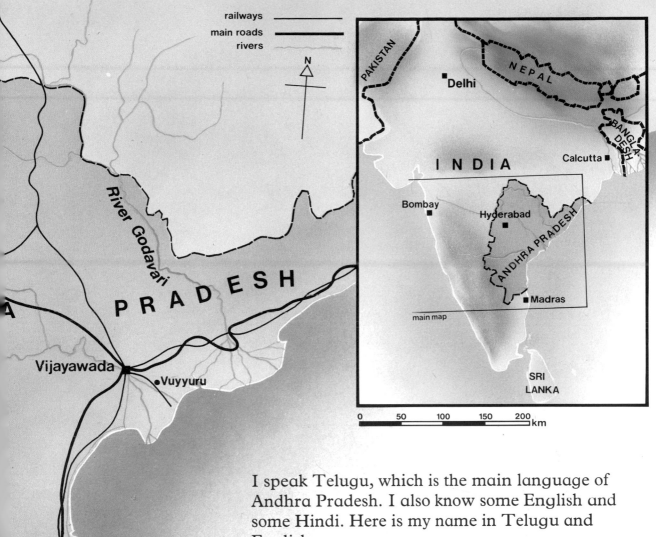

railways
main roads
rivers

I speak Telugu, which is the main language of Andhra Pradesh. I also know some English and some Hindi. Here is my name in Telugu and English.

ప. నారాయణ రెడ్డి

P. Narayana Reddy

P. stands for Pasupula, which is my family name. Everyone in my family has P. in front of their name. I'm quite small for my age, so my family calls me Chinna Narayana Reddy, or just Chinnoda. Chinna means 'small' in Telugu.

3

The nearest town to my village is called Chagalamarry. It's about three kilometres away and is just a small town. This is the main street in Chagalamarry.

There is a dirt track from Chagalamarry to my village. A bus goes into the town and back twice a day. Sometimes I get away with paying half fare on the bus because I'm so small. Lots of people go by bicycle. There is a cycle shop in Chagalamarry where you can rent a bicycle for 30 paisa (1½ pence) an hour.

You can also hire a jutka in Chagalamarry, but that's quite expensive. A jutka is a horse and cart. This jutka and driver have just arrived in my village.

This is the view from the top of our house. The fields are very dry because we don't have much rain. We can only grow crops which need very little water, like peanuts, cotton, millet, lentils, and a type of rice which can grow in dry places.

The rainy season starts in June, when the monsoon winds blow from the Indian Ocean. But sometimes the rains are very light or there is no rain at all. Then a lot of crops die.

The government is going to build a reservoir in the hills behind our village. Then they will dig a canal down to our fields. This means we will be able to store the monsoon rain and irrigate our fields.

My dad is the village munsip. People in the village who own land have to pay money to the government, a bit like paying rates. My dad's job is to collect this money. He is also a member of the village council and helps to organise the business of the village.

Dad owns about thirty acres of land in the village. Some of the people who live here don't have any land of their own. They work for my dad and for other men in the village. Sometimes Dad pays the workers with money and sometimes with rice.

My grandfather is in charge of the people who work in Dad's fields. He gets up very early in the morning, like everyone in our village, so that he can get a lot of work done while it is still cool.

When it gets very hot in the middle of the day, Grandfather sometimes has a rest, and keeps an eye on our oxen. He has brought a bed outside to sit on. Our beds are quite light so that they can be carried around easily.

My dad's mother and father both live with us. My grandmother helps Mum with the housework and the cooking. Our meals are cooked indoors on a wood fire. Today, Mum and Grandmother are making rotis, a kind of flat round bread.

Mum buys some of our food from one of our neighbours in the village. He has a shop in the back room of his house. For special things like soap and cloth, we have to go to Chagalamarry.

Another of Mum's jobs is to milk the buffaloes. They have to be milked twice a day. Mum uses the milk to make curd (yoghurt) and for coffee. She makes delicious coffee!

My brother is three years older than me. His name is the same as mine. But we call him Pedha, which means 'big', so that we don't get mixed up. Pedha Narayana is studying science at the college in Chagalamarry. He cycles there every day.

I have two younger sisters as well. Naga Lakshmi is nine. She likes playing and doesn't like doing school work much.

My other sister is seven. She's named Saradha, after a Telugu film actress. Saradha likes playing, but she likes studying too. I think she's very clever for her age, and she's my favourite sister. Here she's helping my grandmother to shell peanuts.

Our house is on the edge of the village. It has one storey and a flat roof with steps going up to it. It's nice going up on the roof in the evening. Sometimes we sleep up there.

There is a big covered verandah at the front of our house where people in the village often come to sit and talk. We have no bedrooms as we sleep outside all the year round, except when it rains. Then we put our beds under the verandah. It is far too hot to sleep in the house, especially in the summer (from April to June).

All down one side of the house there is a godown (store) for peanuts and rice that have been harvested.

We have electric lights in our house now. Electricity was
brought to our village in 1976. Before that we used kerosene
lamps. We have a kitchen and bathroom in the house, but
there is no running water. We get our drinking water from
pumps and store it in large clay jars. There are several water
pumps in the village. You can see one of them just behind the
oxen cart in the picture.

There are also wells around the village where people get
water to do their washing. Sometimes, when it is very hot,
some of the boys swim in the wells to cool down.

Most of the people in my village are Hindu like us, although there are a few Muslim families too. I'm sitting beside the tulsima shrine outside our house. There are special holy patterns painted on the shrine. A tulsi bush is planted in the top and my mum always hangs her new bangles on the bush to bring her good luck. Lots of Hindu women do this. We have another shrine inside the house, where we pray.

Hindus believe in many gods. One of my favourite gods is Rama. In the evening, Dad sometimes tells us stories about Rama. There is a small temple to Rama in the village.

Up in the hills behind our village there is another temple. It has a shrine with little statues of women wrapped in red cloth. We call the statues akka-chellelu (sister goddesses) and they are special goddesses for our village.

Can you see the chalk pattern on the stone in front of the shrine? It's called muggu in Telugu. Muggu patterns bring good luck, and people often draw them outside the doors of their houses. This woman is putting a muggu pattern outside a temple in a town near my village. There are lots of different muggu patterns.

13

This is the village school in Chinthalacheruvu. It's closed for the summer holidays. The school is run by the government and all the children in the village are supposed to go there. I went to this school until I was ten.

I didn't get on very well at school and did badly in the exams. Sometimes I told my parents I was going to school and then I ran off and played in the fields all day with some of the other village boys. When my father found out, he was very angry.

Then, one day, my parents heard that my uncle, Ranga Reddy, and his wife had started a school in a small town called Vuyyuru. It is in another part of Andhra Pradesh. My uncle said I could study at his school. It's called Vuyyuru Public School. So, three years ago, I came to Vuyyuru to study.

It's a long way to Vuyyuru from my village, so I live with my aunt and uncle and just go home in the school holidays. I was sad to leave my village and my family, but very excited to have the chance to go to Uncle's school.

Vuyyuru is very different from my village. The fields around Vuyyuru are flat and fertile because there are lots of irrigation canals from the River Krishna. The main crops are rice and sugar cane. There are two rice harvests every year.

The sugar cane is harvested from December right through until May. When it is cut down, the cane is loaded onto bullock carts and taken into Vuyyuru. There's a huge sugar factory in Vuyyuru, just down the road from our school, where the cane is processed into sugar.

During the sugar season, Vuyyuru is crowded with carts going to the factory. Sometimes, after school, I go down to the factory with some of my friends and sneak into the yard to take pieces of cane. It's delicious to chew.

This is my aunt and uncle and my cousin at the school in Vuyyuru. My cousin is only five, but she's good fun. We call her Smiley because she's always laughing.

We live in two rooms that are attached to the school building. We eat all our meals in the kitchen. For lunch we are having rice, vegetable curry, yoghurt and dal, which is made of lentils and spices. Occasionally we eat mutton or chicken, but meat is very expensive. We never eat beef because we are Hindu.

All the cooking is done on two kerosene stoves. You can see one in the picture. The big metal container in the corner is for storing rice. Most of our dishes are made of metal, too. We often give people stainless steel dishes as wedding presents as they are quite expensive and last a long time.

School starts with assembly at nine thirty in the morning. We all gather in the school grounds to say prayers and a special poem about India. Aunty is taking assembly this morning. Lessons start straight after assembly. There are seven lessons a day and school finishes at ten past four. We have school on Saturday morning too.

At one o'clock we have an hour's lunch break. I eat my lunch with Aunty and Uncle and Smiley. Some of the children go home for lunch. The others bring their lunch to school in metal boxes and eat it in the school garden.

People have to pay fees to send their children to my uncle's school. The fees are 22 rupees a month (just over £1) and parents pay for all the textbooks, exercise books, pencils and pens, too. We didn't pay fees at my old school because it was run by the government.

In my old school, we didn't have a uniform either, but we do at Vuyyuru. Here are two of my friends, Subha Rao and Gandhi, in their school uniform. They are standing on either side of Narayana, one of the school rickshaw drivers. Children who live a long way from the school come and go in cycle rickshaws.

There are two kindergarten classes in our school. The youngest children in the kindergarten are only three years old. They are practicing their letters in Telugu and English. Can you see the slates on the teacher's desk? They write on the slates with chalk. When they have finished they can rub the letters out and start again.

Apart from kindergarten, there are seven other classes. Smiley is in the first standard. Her class uses proper books. They are having a Telugu lesson and Smiley is sitting in the front row.

There are exams eight times a year. If we fail the big end-of-year exams we have to repeat the year. At the end of the seventh class we have to take a public exam to go on to High School.

When I first came to the school, it was very difficult for me as I was away from home. I've settled down now and I enjoy school. I like working hard. When I grow up I'd like to be a doctor, but whether I'll make it or not I don't know.

I am in the sixth class. My class has lessons on the verandah and we are having an English lesson this morning. We study Maths, Science, English, Telugu, Hindi and Social Studies, which includes the history and geography of India and the world. The teachers are very strict and give us a lot of homework.

After school I often do some shopping for aunty. There's a big market in Vuyyuru where I go to buy fruit and vegetables. This stall is selling limes, oranges and corriander (a kind of spice). Aunty makes a lovely refreshing drink from lime juice.

If I have any money left over, I go to the sweet stall. My favourite sweet is burfi. It's made from milk and sugar.

In the evening, I sometimes go to the cinema with Aunty and Uncle and Smiley. There are five cinemas in Vuyyuru, all showing different films. This is the one right next to the school, called Laxmi Talkies.

It only costs 1 rupee (about 6 pence) to go to the cinema. The films that come to Vuyyuru are either in Hindi or Telugu. Most Indian films are about three hours long, but there is an interval in the middle when you can buy tea and nuts to eat.

Outside the cinema, there are big posters to advertise the films. All the posters are painted by hand. Once, when I went to Vijayawada, our nearest big town, I saw some men painting film posters. This man is painting a famous Telugu film star from a photograph.

23

Every February in Vuyyuru, there's a special festival called the Tirunulla. The festival is dedicated to Veeramma, the special goddess of Vuyyuru. People come from all around Vuyyuru for the festival. Veeramma is also a goddess of fertility and people bring their oxen to the temple to be blessed by the goddess. They put pink powder on the oxen and walk them round the temple three times.

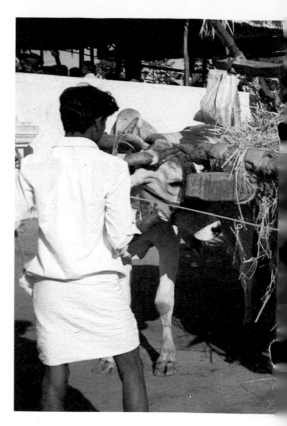

During Tirunulla, lots of stalls and amusements are set up all round the temple. Some of the people who have stalls make their living by travelling from festival to festival. I love going to the temple and seeing all the people.

This year I went with Aunty and Smiley. Aunty bought some toys for Smiley and me, and some new bangles for herself. Smiley had a go on the roundabout, but I'm too old for that now.

The festival lasts for just two weeks. I am always sorry when it's over. The town seems very quiet afterwards. I'm already looking forward to the Tirunullu again next year.